# THE JOURNEY TO BECOMING THE MAN I WAS MEANT TO BE

A Guide to Identity, Accountability, and Transformation

JACOBIE WILLIAMS

In partnership with the *Institute of Research* for Social Justice in Action

# CONTENTS

**INTRODUCTION** . . . . . . . . . . . . . . . . . . . . . . . . . . . . . . . . . . . . . . . . . . . . . . . **5**

**My Story. Your Journey.**

**SECTION 1. IDENTITY — WHO AM I REALLY?** . . . . . . . . . . . . . . . . . . . . . . . . . . . . . . **13**
Breaking false labels, reclaiming self-worth, and understanding who you are beneath your mistakes.

**SECTION 2. THE POWER OF CHOICE** . . . . . . . . . . . . . . . . . . . . . . . . . . . . . . . . . . . . **25**
How every decision shapes your direction and determines the man you are becoming.

**SECTION 3. CIRCLES OF INFLUENCE — WHO ARE YOU WALKING WITH?** . . . . . **39**
Understanding how people, environments, and loyalty shape your outcomes—for better or worse.

**SECTION 4. EMOTIONS, ANGER, AND HEALING — WHAT ARE YOU REALLY FEELING?** . . . . . . . . . . . . . . . . . . . . . . . . . . . . . . . . . . . . . . . . . . . . . . . . . . **53**
Recognizing triggers, managing emotional reactions, and understanding how unresolved pain drives behavior.

**SECTION 5. PURPOSE AND VISION — WHAT ARE YOU LIVING FOR?** . . . . . . . . . . **65**
Facing what you carry, releasing what holds you back, and taking responsibility without shame.

**SECTION 6. RELATIONSHIPS, RESPECT, AND FAMILY — HOW DO YOU SHOW UP FOR OTHERS?** . . . . . . . . . . . . . . . . . . . . . . . . . . . . . . . . . . . . . . . . . . **77**
Seeing beyond your current situation and identifying meaning, direction, and potential in your life.

**SECTION 7. FAITH, MINDSET AND TRANSFORMATION — HOW DO YOU CHANGE FROM THE INSIDE OUT?** . . . . . . . . . . . . . . . . . . . . . . . . . . . . . **89**
Redefining manhood through discipline, character, healthy relationships, and responsibility.

**SECTION 8. MANHOOD, LEADERSHIP, AND NEXT STEPS — WHO WILL YOU BE FROM HERE FORWARD?** . . . . . . . . . . . . . . . . . . . . . . . . . . . . . . . . . . **99**
Taking ownership of your future, building a personal code, and committing to who you choose to become.

# INTRODUCTION

## MY STORY. YOUR JOURNEY.

I didn't grow up knowing who I was meant to be, but I grew up learning very early what I didn't want my life to turn into.

I grew up in Ensley, in the projects on the west side of Birmingham, Alabama. If you know Ensley, you already understand the pressure that comes with it. If you don't, let me explain how it was for me. It was a place where survival mattered more than vision, where the streets introduced you to life fast, and where expectations were often set before you ever had a chance to set them for yourself.

I saw a lot at an early age.

I saw gangs. Crips. Bloods. GDs. I saw hustling, violence, and constant movement. I saw people go to prison and people lose their lives. I saw uncles, neighbors, and friends disappear one way or another. None of that felt unusual. It felt normal. And when something becomes normal, it starts shaping how you think—about success, about manhood, about what's worth chasing.

I also grew up in a big family.

Six siblings, four brothers and two sisters.

And when you grow up like that, you learn early that everybody doesn't stand out the same way. Not everyone gets the same attention. Not everyone is automatically seen as 'the one.' I wasn't the one who looked the best. I wasn't the one who had the most. I wasn't the one people naturally pointed to and said, "That's him right there."

So from early on, I was trying to figure out where I fit.

When you don't know who you are yet, you start paying close attention to who seems respected. Who seems powerful. Who looks like they've figured life out. And in my world, the people who looked like they had it figured out were the dudes in the streets.

They had money and cars. They had clothes, influence, and attention.

That was the picture of success I saw every day. So I became infatuated with that image. Not because I wanted destruction or because I wanted to throw my life away. Because I wanted something.

I wanted to matter. I wanted to feel like I belonged somewhere. I wanted what I thought success looked like. When that's all you see, you start equating money with worth. You start equating status with manhood and hustle with intelligence. And without even realizing it, you begin to emulate what you admire. So I learned from the streets and from the people I watched. I learned from what looked respected and powerful at the time.

At the same time, there was a gap in my life that I didn't fully understand until later.

My father was incarcerated when I was born and stayed incarcerated throughout my childhood. I didn't really meet him until I was around nineteen years old, when I was in college. That meant I grew up without consistent male guidance. No daily example of how to handle pressure or a steady voice teaching me how to make decisions or what manhood actually looked like.

So, like a lot of people, I figured it out as I went.

But my life wasn't one-dimensional. I went to school. I had structure. And for a long time, I had hope because of basketball. Ball gave me discipline. It gave me confidence and something to believe in. It made me feel like there was a way out—like my story didn't have to end where it started.

I also had proof that making it out was possible. One of my brothers made it to the NFL. That mattered. That wasn't a fantasy—it was real. It showed me that success wasn't just something you saw on TV. Talent, opportunity, and discipline could actually change a family's story. So in many ways, I did make it out physically.

But here's the part people don't always talk about. Even when I left physically, my mindset stayed in the streets. I carried the same thinking into new environments. I responded to pressure the same way. I looked at money the same way. I looked at respect the same way. I had access to new spaces, but I was still moving with an old definition of success.

So when opportunities came that matched that mindset, I leaned into them. And for a while, it worked. I was doing my thing. I was making money. I was connected. I had a nightclub, and I was bringing in artists. I was living a life that, on the outside, looked successful. People respected me and knew my name. I had access, influence, and status.

By the standards I had grown up with, I had "made it."

But here's the truth I had to face: I was chasing something, and when I finally caught it, it wasn't what I thought it would be.

I had the money.

The lifestyle.

The attention.

And still, something was missing.

I couldn't ignore the feeling that the road I was on was leading somewhere I didn't want to end up. I couldn't ignore the people around me who weren't right. I couldn't ignore the patterns I was repeating. And I couldn't ignore the fact that success built on shaky ground always comes with a cost.

And I knew something else, too. I didn't want my story to mirror my father's. I didn't want to spend years of my life locked away, and for my future children to grow up knowing me through stories instead of in person. I didn't want the same cycle to keep repeating itself through another generation.

The Bible teaches us that warning comes before destruction.

Looking back now, I can see the warnings clearly. Moments that should have slowed me down. Situations that should have made me think. Close calls that were telling me to stop playing with fire.

But the loudest warning came in the form of an accident. A serious accident that could have ended my life. That moment stopped everything. It stripped away the noise, the lifestyle, the image, the chasing. In that moment, none of it mattered. All that mattered was the reality that I was still alive—and that I easily could not have been.

And in that space, I had a real conversation with God.

Not a rehearsed prayer or something I had heard someone else say. Just honesty.

I had to ask myself why I was still here. Why my life had been spared. Why I kept being given chances when the road I was on was clearly dangerous.

And the answer wasn't dramatic—but it was clear. I was still here because my life was meant for more than survival. More than money or reputation, and more than chasing things that never truly satisfied me.

That's when I made a decision.

Not a promise made out of fear.

A decision.

I decided I didn't want to keep living on borrowed time or keep flirting with destruction. I decided that if God had spared my life, I wasn't going to waste it chasing things that were never going to fulfill me anyway.

I decided to serve God—not just with words, but with how I lived.

That decision didn't instantly fix everything. It didn't erase my past. But it changed my direction. It changed how I thought and how I made decisions. It taught me that discipline isn't about restriction. It's about alignment. And that accountability isn't punishment—it's freedom.

Choosing to make that decision didn't instantly change things. In fact, some of the hardest parts came later. I had to humble myself.

Coming from a hustler's lifestyle, that wasn't easy. I had been used to moving fast. I had been used to making real money. I had been used to a certain level of control and respect. So when it came time to actually live differently, that meant letting go of the image I had built and accepting a season that didn't look impressive.

I had to go get a real job.

I remember taking a job with a security company, and if I'm being honest, it felt low at first. Going from making tens of thousands of dollars a month to that kind of paycheck messes with your pride. It makes you question yourself, like you're starting over from scratch.

But what I didn't realize at the time was that every step of humility was also a step of rebuilding. With every sacrifice, I gained something I never had before.

I gained integrity.

I learned how to show up consistently, even when it wasn't glamorous. I learned how to build something the right way instead of the fast way. And I learned that real growth often feels like loss before it feels like gain.

That season taught me something I carry with me to this day: Humbling yourself isn't losing—it's laying a foundation. And eventually, that foundation led me to my purpose.

Out of that season came the work I do now. Out of obedience, sacrifice, and humility came my community organization. What started as me choosing to do the right thing eventually turned into me being able to serve my community, save lives, and build something rooted in purpose instead of ego.

I learned that real change doesn't happen because something scares you. It happens because you decide to listen.

The accident didn't change my life by itself.

Faith didn't change my life by itself.

Opportunity didn't change my life by itself.

The decision did.

And once my mindset began to change, my purpose became clearer. I started seeing how many people were walking around with the same potential I had—but without direction. People who weren't broken. People who weren't hopeless. People who just needed help seeing themselves differently.

Today, people call me a hometown hero. I'm known for saving lives, building peace, and restoring community. My organization, Everybody W.E.N.S., works closely with city leadership and the mayor's office. I'm respected now not for fear or reputation, but for impact and service.

But what matters most to me is this:

I didn't lose my influence. I redirected it. And I'm here because I believe the same potential that was in me is in you.

You were born to be more than what the streets labeled you. More than your mistakes. More than the version of yourself you had to become just to survive.

Over the next eight weeks, we're going to slow down and really look at the places where many of us fell short. Not to shame ourselves—but to understand ourselves. We're going to examine the decisions, the thinking, the pressure, and the beliefs that shaped our paths.

Because growth happens by understanding.

This is a journey back to yourself. Back to the part of you that existed before survival took over. Back to the part of you that still knows you were meant for more.

You were born to be great. You were born with value. You were born to become a good man—not the version shaped by pressure or pain, but the one rooted in purpose, discipline, and clarity.

If you're willing to do the work, to reflect honestly, and to make different decisions moving forward, this journey can help you evolve into a greater version of yourself. Not the person you had to be to survive, but the person you were always meant to become.

Let's begin.

# HOW THIS BOOK IS MEANT TO BE USED

This book was written to be more than a story and more than a motivational read. It was designed to be a tool for growth, whether that growth happens in a prison classroom, a community space, a small group, or quietly on your own.

There is no single "right" way to use this book. What matters most is honesty, consistency, and willingness.

## A Flexible Guide

This book can be used in multiple ways:

- As a group-based curriculum in prisons, reentry programs, community organizations, or faith-based spaces
- As a facilitated learning tool led by mentors, coaches, counselors, or community leaders
- As an individual reflection guide for men who are doing the work privately and at their own pace

Each chapter builds on the last, but readers are encouraged to move through the material at their own pace, in line with their environment, responsibilities, and readiness.

## Growth Work Is the Work

Throughout the book, you'll find sections labeled Growth Work. They are where real change happens.

The Growth Work is designed to:

- Slow you down
- Help you reflect honestly
- Identify patterns
- Take responsibility without shame
- Begin making intentional decisions

Whether you are in a group or reading on your own, it's strongly encouraged that you write your responses, revisit them, and reflect on them over time.

## Individual or Group Use

If you are using this book in a group setting, the chapters and Growth Work can be used as a foundation for discussion and reflection.

If you are using this book independently, you are encouraged to take your time and consider each exercise deeply.

Some chapters may take longer than others. That's normal.

## A Note on Honesty and Accountability

This book will only work if you tell yourself the truth. There is no benefit in performing, pretending, or writing what sounds good. Growth begins when honesty replaces defense.

## Moving Forward

You don't need to have everything figured out before you begin. You just need to be willing to look at yourself clearly and choose differently when the opportunity comes.

Whether this book meets you in a classroom, a cell, a community space, or a quiet moment alone, the work is the same.

And the decision is always yours.

# CHAPTER ONE

# IDENTITY — WHO AM I REALLY?

Let's start with something honest.

Most of us spend our lives trying to change what we do without ever stopping to understand who we believe ourselves to be. And that's why the same patterns keep showing up. Different situations, same outcomes. Different environments, same decisions.

That's not because people don't want to change. It's because behavior doesn't lead identity — identity leads behavior. Before you ever made a choice that cost you something, you had already decided, consciously or not, who you were allowed to be. And once that identity settles in, everything else lines up behind it.

So if we're serious about growth, we can't start with rules, habits, or discipline. We have to start with the foundation.

We have to talk about identity.

## HOW IDENTITY REALLY FORMS

Identity is not something you're born understanding. It's something you absorb.

From the time you're young, you're watching everything:

- Who gets attention
- Who gets respected
- Who gets protected
- Who gets ignored

You're learning what matters long before anyone explains it to you.

And when you grow up in environments where survival is the priority, identity gets shaped around survival. You don't wake up one day and say, "I'm going to become this kind of man." You slowly adapt to what keeps you safe, what keeps you relevant, what keeps you from feeling small.

That adaptation feels normal. Necessary, even.

But normal doesn't mean true.

## WHY SO MANY OF US STRUGGLE WITH IDENTITY

Growing up as one of seven siblings taught me something early: when attention is divided, identity gets competitive. You start measuring yourself without realizing it.

Who's the strongest?

Who's the smartest?

Who's the one people talk about?

And when you don't feel like you're winning in those categories, you start searching for another way to matter. That search is where identity confusion begins. Not because you're broken, but because you're human. When no one clearly tells you who you are, you start letting your environment answer that question for you. And environments speak in examples.

You become what you see rewarded.

## ADAPTATION IS NOT THE SAME AS IDENTITY

This is where many people get stuck.

We confuse adaptation with identity.

Adaptation says:

> "This is who I have to be to survive here."

Identity says:

> "This is who I am, no matter where I am."

The problem is that adaptation works only in the short term. It helps you fit in. It helps you stay protected or navigate dangerous or unstable spaces. But when adaptation becomes permanent, it starts costing you.

You carry survival habits into spaces where they no longer serve you. You keep reacting instead of choosing and performing instead of becoming. And eventually, you wake up realizing you've been loyal to a version of yourself that kept you alive, but never helped you grow.

## A DIFFERENT LENS: TWO BROTHERS, SAME QUESTION

Let me slow this down and make it plain.

One brother grows up with very little. Single-parent household. Multiple siblings and limited guidance. He learns early that attention is scarce, and respect has to be taken.

Another brother grows up with more stability. Two parents. Bills paid and food on the table. But emotionally, he's invisible. No affirmation. No real conversation. Just expectations.

On paper, their lives look different.

Internally, they're asking the same question:

Who am I, really?

So both adapt.

One adapts by becoming hard. One adapts by becoming distant.

One adapts by hustling. One adapts by numbing himself.

Different expressions. Same root. Identity confusion doesn't come from one type of background. It comes from not being seen clearly.

## WHEN IDENTITY STARTS RUNNING YOUR LIFE

Here's the part people don't like to confront. Once identity is formed, it starts filtering everything:

- How you interpret respect
- How you handle pressure
- How you respond to authority
- How you define success
- How you justify decisions

You don't just make choices — you make identity-consistent choices.

If you believe you're disposable, you'll live recklessly.

If you believe you're only valuable when you're useful, you'll overextend.

If you believe you're dangerous, you'll keep proving it.

And you won't even realize that identity is the engine underneath it all.

## WHY GOD'S DEFINITION MATTERS

This is where Scripture interrupts the whole conversation.

Jeremiah 1:5 says:

> "I knew you before I formed you in your mother's womb."

That verse is disruptive. It tells us identity didn't start in your neighborhood or in your household. It didn't start with your worst moment.

It started with intention.

Which means:

- Your trauma didn't create you

- Your mistakes didn't define you
- Your environment didn't name you

They influenced you, but they did not author you. That distinction matters. Because if identity comes from God, then identity is something you return to, not something you invent.

## WHAT REAL IDENTITY WORK LOOKS LIKE

Identity work is more than affirmations. It's an honest examination.

It's asking:

- What version of myself did I become just to survive?
- What beliefs did I adopt without questioning?
- What parts of me are adaptation — not truth?

That process is uncomfortable. It requires humility and slowing down. It requires letting go of images that once protected you. But it's necessary. Because until identity is clarified, growth will always be fragile.

## WHY THIS CHAPTER COMES FIRST

We don't start this journey with choices. We don't start with discipline or with manhood. We start here because identity is the foundation everything else sits on.

If identity is unclear, discipline feels like punishment and growth feels like loss. If identity is unclear, change feels threatening. But when identity is grounded, everything else starts to make sense.

## THE QUESTION YOU CAN'T AVOID

So before we go any further, there's one question that matters more than any other: Who have you been living as, and who did you never get the space to become?

That question isn't meant to shame you. It's meant to wake you up. Because identity is not about who you've been. It's about who you're willing to return to.

And that's where this journey really begins.

# GROWTH WORK — CHAPTER ONE

## IDENTITY: WHO AM I REALLY?

This work requires honest answers. You don't have to share this with anyone unless you choose to. But you do owe yourself the truth.

Take your time. Sit with each question. Write what comes up, not what sounds good.

## PART ONE: THE IDENTITY YOU LEARNED

Before you ever decided who you wanted to be, life was already teaching you who to become.

1. **Growing up, what did "success" look like around you?**

   Think about what you saw rewarded in your home, your neighborhood, your school, or your circle.

   What did people respect?

   What did people fear?

   What did people chase?

   Write honestly.

2. **Who were the people you watched the most growing up?**

These could be family members, older guys in the neighborhood, athletes, hustlers, entertainers, or anyone you paid attention to.

Why do you think you watched them?

____________________________________________________________

____________________________________________________________

____________________________________________________________

____________________________________________________________

____________________________________________________________

3. **What traits did you start copying, even without realizing it?**

Examples might include:

- How you handle anger
- How you deal with conflict
- How you talk to people
- How you see money, respect, or authority

____________________________________________________________

____________________________________________________________

____________________________________________________________

____________________________________________________________

____________________________________________________________

## PART TWO: ADAPTATION VS. IDENTITY

Some parts of who you are today were learned just to survive. They may not be as helpful now, but they are not permanent either.

4. **What version of yourself did you become just to survive your environment?**

   Be specific. This might include being hard, quiet, reckless, funny, distant, aggressive, or always "on guard."

   ________________________________________

   ________________________________________

   ________________________________________

   ________________________________________

   ________________________________________

5. **Which of those traits protected you at one time, but may be holding you back now?**

   This is where honesty matters most.

   ________________________________________

   ________________________________________

   ________________________________________

   ________________________________________

   ________________________________________

## PART THREE: THE IDENTITY YOU BELIEVED

Identity is more than how you act. It's what you believe about yourself.

6. **Complete these sentences honestly:**

   - Growing up, I believed I was ______________________________.
   - Deep down, I feared I was ______________________________.

- I felt most unseen when ______________________________.

______________________________

______________________________

______________________________

______________________________

______________________________

7. **What labels have followed you — spoken or unspoken?**

   These could be things people called you, expected from you, or assumed about you. Which ones did you start believing?

   ______________________________

   ______________________________

   ______________________________

   ______________________________

   ______________________________

## PART FOUR: INTERRUPTING THE OLD STORY

Scripture says God knew you before your environment ever did. That means some of what you believe about yourself needs to be challenged.

8. **What parts of your identity do you believe came from pain, pressure, or survival — not purpose?**

   ______________________________

   ______________________________

   ______________________________

   ______________________________

   ______________________________

9. **If your environment had not shaped you first, who do you think you might have become?**

   Try not to focus on regret or blame. This is about awareness.

## PART FIVE: LOOKING FORWARD

Identity is flexible, and we can build a new one if we choose.

10. **Write one sentence describing the man you are becoming — not perfectly, but intentionally.**

    Start with:

    "I am becoming a man who..."

## CLOSING REFLECTION

Take a moment and read what you wrote. Notice patterns of honesty or resistance.

You don't need to fix anything yet. This chapter was to help you see clearly. Because once you see yourself honestly, change stops being confusing and becomes possible.

Identity is the foundation. Everything else builds from here.

When you're ready, move forward.

# CHAPTER TWO

# THE POWER OF CHOICE

If identity answers the question "Who am I?" then choice answers the question "What am I going to do about it?" This is where things get real.

Most men don't struggle with understanding right and wrong. We struggle at the moment where pressure meets opportunity and old habits feel easier than new discipline. We struggle when the choice in front of us costs something immediately, even if it saves us later.

That's why this chapter matters.

## THE LIE WE LEARN EARLY

Growing up where many of us grew up, it often felt like life made the decisions for us.

The block made the decision.

Poverty made the decision.

Violence made the decision.

Broken systems made the decision.

After a while, that pressure trains you to believe something dangerous: "This is just how life is. I don't really have a choice."

But that belief quietly robs you of responsibility, and responsibility is where power lives. The truth is this: You may not have chosen your starting point, but you are always choosing your direction. God made that clear.

Deuteronomy 30:19 says,

> "Today I have given you the choice between life and death... Oh, that you would choose life!"

That verse doesn't deny reality or pretend pressure isn't real. It simply tells the truth: choice still exists, even when life is hard.

## CHOICE IS WHERE YOUR FUTURE GETS BUILT

Most people think big moments change your life.

They don't.

Your life is built through repeated decisions, made when nobody's watching, when nobody's clapping, and when the right choice doesn't feel powerful — it feels costly.

A choice got me into some of my darkest situations.

A choice put me around people I shouldn't have trusted.

A choice cost me time, peace, and opportunities I didn't even realize I was risking.

But another choice — a different one — started pulling me out. That's something I had to learn the hard way: You don't become a better man by accident.

You become one by decision at a time.

## CASE STUDY: THE PHONE CALL

There's a moment a lot of us know too well. Your phone rings. You already know who it is.

It's familiar. It's connected to the old version of you. Fast money. Old habits. Chaos you know how to manage. It represents relief — not growth, but relief.

You've been trying to do better. Trying to think differently. Trying to move with more discipline. But this call feels easy.

You tell yourself:

"It's just this one time."

"I need the money."

"I can handle it."

That's where choice actually lives. Not when consequences show up or when things fall apart. Right there.

One man answers the phone.

Nothing bad happens immediately. In fact, things feel smoother for a moment. Stress goes down. Confidence comes back. Money comes fast.

But the door he was slowly closing swings wide open again.

Old patterns return.

Old circles tighten.

Old consequences start forming quietly.

Another man sees the phone ring... and lets it ring.

That choice feels weak at first. It feels like loss. It feels like starting over. It feels like he's walking away from something familiar without knowing what's coming next.

Nothing dramatic happens.

But something important does.

Direction changes.

## EVERY CHOICE IS A SEED

Here's something I wish I understood earlier.

Every choice you make is a seed. Some seeds grow fast, and some take time. But none of them disappear.

When you choose anger, it grows into distance.

When you choose avoidance, it grows into stagnation.

When you choose comfort, it grows into limitation.

And when you choose accountability, it grows into strength.

When you choose discipline, it grows into stability.

When you choose God, it grows into alignment.

You don't get to choose whether seeds grow.

You only get to choose what you plant.

## THE TRAP OF NOT CHOOSING

Many men think avoiding a decision keeps them safe.

It doesn't. Not choosing is still choosing.

Choosing not to leave a situation is a choice.

Choosing not to change a habit is a choice.

Choosing not to take responsibility is a choice.

Avoidance doesn't protect you from consequences; it delays them. And delayed consequences usually come heavier.

## CHOICE REVEALS WHO YOU'RE BECOMING

Your choices tell the truth, even when your words don't.

They reveal:

- What you value
- What you fear
- What you're committed to
- What direction you're really moving in

You can't keep choosing destruction and expect peace.

You can't keep choosing distraction and expect purpose.

You can't keep choosing comfort and expect growth.

That's not judgment. That's reality.

## WHY HUMILITY IS PART OF RIGHT CHOICES

Sometimes the right choice doesn't feel strong. It feels humbling.

Choosing differently meant letting go of pride. It meant starting over. It meant going from fast money to honest work. It meant taking jobs that didn't match the image I once had of myself.

I'm not going to lie — that messes with your head. But humility taught me something pride never could: consistency.

And consistency built what shortcuts never could.

## WHY THIS CHAPTER COMES AFTER IDENTITY

Once you start understanding who you really are, your choices become clearer. Not easier, but clearer.

When identity is unclear, discipline feels like punishment. When identity is grounded, discipline feels like alignment. You stop asking, "What can I get away with?" and start asking, "Does this move me closer to who I'm becoming?"

That shift changes everything.

## ONE CHOICE CAN CHANGE THE DIRECTION

People say, "Your future is one choice away."

That's not a slogan. That's truth.

One choice to walk away.

One choice to ask for help.

One choice to stop pretending.

One choice to break a pattern.

One choice to say, "I'm not living like this anymore."

Those choices don't just affect you. They affect generations.

## WHERE THIS LEAVES YOU

You don't have to fix your whole life today. But you do have to decide the direction. Every man reaches a moment where he realizes: "If I keep choosing like this, I already know where it leads."

Another road is always available. Not because life is fair or easy, but because God gave you the power to choose.

And when you choose life — intentionally, consistently, and honestly — everything else starts to follow.

## CLOSING TRUTH

You don't change your whole life at once. But you can change the direction of your whole life with one decision.

Choose life.

Choose growth.

Choose to become the man you were created to be.

And then keep choosing it, one day at a time.

# GROWTH WORK — CHAPTER TWO

## THE POWER OF CHOICE

Ownership is growth, not blame.

Take your time. Read each section carefully before writing.

## PART ONE: THE ILLUSION OF "NO CHOICE"

Many of us learned early to believe that life decided for us. This section will help name where that belief came from.

1. **Growing up, where did you feel like you didn't have a choice?**

   Think about moments where you felt boxed in by:

   - Environment
   - Poverty
   - Violence
   - Family expectations
   - Fear
   - Survival

   Write what felt unavoidable at the time.

2. **What choices did you tell yourself you had to make?**

   Examples:

   - "I had to hustle."
   - "I had to react."
   - "I had to move a certain way."
   - "I had to stay loyal."

   Be honest about the story you told yourself.

## PART TWO: THE MOMENT BEFORE THE DECISION

Every major outcome starts before the action. This section will identify that moment.

3. **Think about a decision that led to consequences in your life.**

   Don't focus on the outcome yet. Focus on the moment before you acted.

   What were you feeling?

   What pressure were you under?

   What were you afraid of losing?

4. **What did you already know in that moment — even if you ignored it?**

   Most people know when a choice is wrong. They just talk themselves out of listening.

   What truth did you push aside?

## PART THREE: THE SEEDS YOU'VE PLANTED

Choices don't disappear. They grow.

Recognizing patterns leads to better outcomes.

5. **What choices do you see repeating in your life?**

   These can be patterns with:

   - Anger
   - Money
   - Relationships
   - Authority
   - Avoidance

- Comfort

______________________________________________

______________________________________________

______________________________________________

______________________________________________

______________________________________________

6. **What have those repeated choices produced so far?**

   Be specific. Don't generalize.

______________________________________________

______________________________________________

______________________________________________

______________________________________________

______________________________________________

## PART FOUR: HUMILITY AND COST

Right choices often cost something immediately. This section is about facing that cost.

7. **What right choice have you avoided because it felt too uncomfortable or humbling?**

   Examples:

   - Walking away
   - Asking for help
   - Starting over
   - Taking responsibility
   - Being patient

8. **What do you think that choice would cost you right now?**

   Name it honestly: pride, image, money, relationships, control.

## PART FIVE: CHOOSING DIRECTION

You don't need to change everything. You just need to change direction.

9. **What is one choice you already know you need to make?**

   Not ten.

   One.

10. **What version of yourself does that choice move you toward?**

    Describe the man on the other side of that decision.

## PART SIX: COMMITMENT WITHOUT PROMISES

You don't need vows or big statements. Just strive for clarity.

11. **Finish this sentence honestly:**

    "If I keep choosing the way I have been choosing, my life will..."

12. **Finish this sentence intentionally:**

    "If I choose differently starting now, my life can..."

## CLOSING REFLECTION

Read what you wrote.

Notice patterns.

Notice fear.

Notice clarity.

You don't have to fix everything today, but now you know this: You are not stuck. You are choosing. And every new choice is a chance to change direction.

Carry this truth with you as you move forward.

Choice is power, so use it wisely.

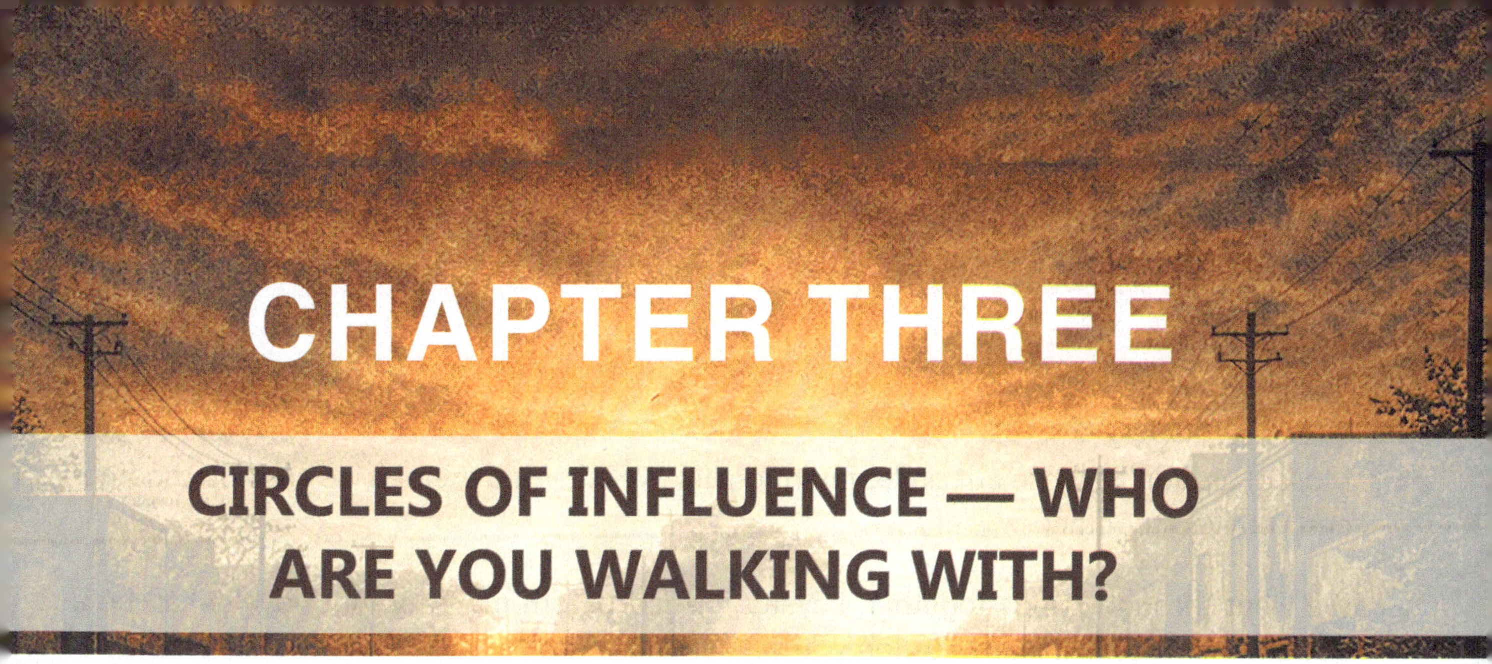

# CHAPTER THREE

## CIRCLES OF INFLUENCE — WHO ARE YOU WALKING WITH?

Let me say this plainly.

A lot of men don't fail because they don't want better. They fail because they're still surrounded by the same voices that shaped the old version of them.

You can decide to change. You can want something different and you can even start moving in the right direction. But if your circle stays the same, your growth will always be under pressure.

Understand your influences, not just who you hang around, but who has access to your thinking, your emotions, and your decisions. Because nobody becomes who they're becoming alone.

### WHY CIRCLES MATTER MORE THAN MOTIVATION

Motivation is internal. Influence is environmental.

You can be motivated and still get pulled backwards. You can be determined and still make decisions that don't match your goals — not because you're weak, but because influence works quietly.

Influence doesn't usually tell you what to do. It shapes what feels normal. If everyone around you treats chaos as normal, peace will feel strange. If everyone around you avoids responsibility, discipline will feel extreme.

If everyone around you is stuck, growth will feel lonely.

That's not a coincidence.

That's influence.

## HOW CIRCLES GET FORMED

Most of us didn't choose our circles intentionally. We inherited them as we grew up together and survived together.

We went through things together. Loyalty formed before maturity. And loyalty can be a good thing — until it starts costing you your future.

A lot of men confuse loyalty with obligation. They stay connected to people not because the relationship is healthy, but because "that's who I came up with."

But who you came up with is not always who you're meant to grow with.

## THE INVISIBLE PRESSURE OF THE CIRCLE

Pressure doesn't always look like someone telling you to do something wrong.

Sometimes it sounds like:

- "You changed."
- "You too good now?"
- "It ain't that serious."
- "Just this one time."

That pressure hits harder when you're already trying to do better. Because now you're not just choosing growth, you're risking relationships. That's where most people fold.

Not because they don't know better, but because they don't want to stand alone.

## CASE STUDY: THE FRIDAY NIGHT

This one is familiar.

Two men grow up together. Same block. Same history. Same struggles. Same memories.

They both say they want better.

Friday night comes.

One man decides to go home. He's tired. He's trying to stay focused. He's thinking about what he's building, even if it's slow.

The other man wants to hang out. Nothing planned, nothing specific — just familiar movement.

He says, "Come on, it's not that deep."

That's the moment.

One man goes.

Nothing wild happens right away. They laugh. They talk. They feel connected again. It feels normal. Comfortable.

But comfort has a cost.

The conversation shifts. Old ideas come back. Old habits feel close again. And slowly, the direction he was moving in starts to blur.

The other man goes home. It doesn't feel exciting. It doesn't feel rewarding. It feels quiet. Almost lonely.

But that night protects something.

Momentum.

One man chose comfort. The other chose clarity.

Both choices felt small.

Only one protected the future.

## WHY GROWTH CREATES DISTANCE

Here's something nobody warns you about. When you start growing, distance happens.

Not because you think you're better. Not because you're judging anyone. But because alignment changes. Your priorities shift. Your conversations and your tolerance for chaos shifts.

And people notice. Some will respect it. Some will resist it and will try to pull you back to what's familiar.

That's when you have to decide:

Am I building a future... or protecting a past?

## CIRCLES DON'T JUST INFLUENCE ACTION — THEY SHAPE THINKING

Your circle affects:

- How you define success
- What you normalize
- How you talk to yourself
- What you tolerate
- What you believe is possible

If everyone around you is stuck, stagnation will feel normal. If everyone around you avoids accountability, growth will feel uncomfortable.

That's why changing circles does not mean cutting people off aggressively. It's about protecting direction.

## THE DIFFERENCE BETWEEN LOYALTY AND ALIGNMENT

Loyalty says:

> "I'm here no matter what."

Alignment says:

"We're moving in the same direction."

You can love people and still outgrow proximity. You can respect someone and still create space, and you don't owe everyone access to your future.

That doesn't make you fake. It makes you intentional.

## WHY THIS CHAPTER COMES AFTER CHOICE

This chapter comes third for a reason.

Once you start choosing differently, your circle will react.

Some will support you.

Some will test you.

Some will resent the change.

Knowing this ahead of time matters.

Because if you don't prepare for circle pressure, you'll misinterpret it as failure.

It's not failure.

It's transition.

## WHAT REAL CIRCLE CHANGE LOOKS LIKE

Changing your circle doesn't always mean new people immediately.

Sometimes it means:

- Spending less time in certain spaces
- Having fewer conversations that go nowhere
- Limiting access to your decision-making
- Being okay with quiet seasons

Growth is often quieter than survival.

And that quiet is where clarity gets built.

## THE TRUTH TO CARRY FORWARD

You cannot build a new life with old influences. You can't keep walking in the same circles and expect a different destination.

This chapter does not ask you to judge your people. Simply guard your future. Because who you walk with will always affect where you end up.

Choose your circle carefully. Your life depends on it.

# GROWTH WORK — CHAPTER THREE

## CIRCLES AND INFLUENCE: WHO ARE YOU WALKING WITH?

This work is about awareness. You don't need to judge anyone or make announcements.

You just need to tell yourself the truth.

Take your time.

## PART ONE: MAPPING YOUR CIRCLE

Everyone has a circle, whether they've named it or not.

1. **List the people you spend the most time with or talk to the most.**

   These can be:

   - Friends
   - Family
   - Associates
   - Cellmates
   - Co-workers
   - Old contacts who still have access to you

   Write names or initials if that feels safer.

2. **Next to each person, write one word that describes how they influence you.**

Examples:

Supportive

Draining

Neutral

Tempting

Motivating

Negative

Challenging

## PART TWO: NORMALIZATION CHECK

Influence works by making things feel normal.

3. **What behaviors feel "normal" in your circle that you know aren't helping you grow?**

Be honest. No explanations needed.

4. **What kind of behavior would feel "weird" or uncomfortable to do around your circle?**

   Examples:

   - Talking about goals
   - Saying no
   - Choosing peace
   - Walking away
   - Setting boundaries

## PART THREE: PRESSURE POINTS

Pressure doesn't always look aggressive. Often it's subtle.

5. **What phrases or reactions from others make you second-guess your growth?**

   Examples:

   - "You changed."
   - "It's not that serious."

- "Just this one time."
- Silence or sarcasm when you do better.

6. **When that pressure shows up, how do you usually respond?**

   Do you:

   - Go along to keep the peace?
   - Pull back quietly?
   - Get defensive?
   - Abandon your plan?

## PART FOUR: LOYALTY VS. ALIGNMENT

Not everyone you love is aligned with where you're going.

7. **Who do you feel loyal to, even when being around them costs you progress?**

   This is honesty, not judgment.

8. **What direction is that relationship actually pulling you toward?**

   Forward?

   Stuck?

   Backwards?

## PART FIVE: PROTECTING YOUR DIRECTION

Growth often requires space.

9. **What boundaries do you need to start setting, even if they feel uncomfortable?**

   Examples:

   - Less time
   - Fewer conversations
   - No certain topics
   - No certain situations

10. **What kind of people or voices do you need more access to right now?**

Examples:

- Accountability
- Honesty
- Stability
- Faith
- Discipline
- Vision

## PART SIX: COMMITMENT TO CLARITY

You don't need to cut everyone off, but you do need to choose your direction.

11. **Finish this sentence honestly:**

"If I stay in the same circles, my life will..."

12. **12. Finish this sentence intentionally:**

"If I protect my direction, my life can..."

## CLOSING REFLECTION

Read what you wrote.

Notice patterns.

And know this: Your circle is shaping your future, whether you admit it or not.

Choose wisely who gets access to your life. Growth requires protection.

# CHAPTER FOUR

# EMOTIONS, ANGER, AND HEALING — WHAT ARE YOU REALLY FEELING?

Let me start here. A lot of us were never taught how to feel. We were taught how to react.

Growing up, emotions were either ignored, laughed at, or punished. If you were hurt, you were told to toughen up. If you were angry, people paid attention. If you were scared, you learned to hide it.

So over time, one emotion became acceptable.

Anger.

Anger felt strong and respected. Anger felt like control. But anger is rarely the real emotion. It's usually the cover.

## WHAT ANGER IS REALLY DOING

Most men think anger is the problem. It's not. Anger is a signal. It's an alarm that something beneath the surface hasn't been addressed.

Under anger, you'll usually find:

- Hurt that was never acknowledged
- Fear you didn't know how to name
- Shame you learned to hide

- Disappointment you never processed
- Loss you were told to "get over"

But since nobody gave us language for those feelings, anger became the default response.

It's fast and familiar. And it keeps people from getting too close.

## WHY ANGER FEELS SAFER THAN HEALING

Healing requires vulnerability. Anger requires none.

When you're angry, you don't have to explain yourself. You don't have to admit pain. You don't have to revisit old wounds. You don't have to sit with uncomfortable truths.

Anger lets you stay armored. And when you grow up in survival mode, armor feels necessary. But here's the truth a lot of us learn too late: Armor that protects you from pain also blocks growth.

## HOW UNPROCESSED EMOTIONS SHOW UP

When emotions don't get processed, they don't disappear. They leak.

They show up as:

- Explosions over small things
- Shutting down during real conversations
- Constant irritation
- Distrust of people who care about you
- Self-sabotage when things start going well

You might not even know why you're reacting the way you are. You just know it feels familiar. That familiarity is unresolved emotion running the show.

## CASE STUDY: THE DISRESPECT MOMENT

This one hits close.

A man is trying to do better. He's changed some habits. He's trying to move differently. He's more aware now.

Then it happens.

Someone says something sideways.

A tone.

A look.

A comment that feels disrespectful.

Immediately, something rises up. His chest tightens. His mind races. Old instincts wake up. He feels that pull to react — to prove something, to assert control, to remind someone who they're dealing with.

That's the moment.

One man reacts.

Words get sharp. The situation escalates. Pride feels satisfied for a moment. But damage is done — relationships strained, consequences set in motion, progress shaken.

But what if that man pauses?

Not because he's weak, but because he's aware. He realizes the anger isn't just about the comment. It's connected to years of being overlooked, talked down to, or disrespected. He takes a breath. He creates space and chooses not to react.

Nothing dramatic happens. But something powerful does.

Control shifts.

## THE DIFFERENCE BETWEEN REACTION AND RESPONSE

Reaction is automatic. Response is intentional.

Reaction is driven by emotion without awareness. Response is driven by emotion with control. You don't lose emotion when you grow. You gain mastery over it.

And that mastery doesn't come from suppression. It comes from understanding.

## WHY HEALING IS A PROCESS

Healing doesn't mean pretending things didn't hurt. But it does mean finally telling the truth about what did.

A lot of us carry things we never talked about:

- Abandonment
- Betrayal
- Violence
- Neglect
- Humiliation

Many of us learned to survive by burying it. But buried pain doesn't stay quiet forever. It waits for moments of stress. Moments of pressure or vulnerability.

That's when it surfaces, and usually through anger.

## WHAT HEALING ACTUALLY REQUIRES

Healing requires:

- Honesty with yourself
- Patience with the process
- Accountability for your reactions

- Safe spaces to tell the truth
- Willingness to feel what you've been avoiding

None of that is easy, but all of it is necessary. Because unhealed pain doesn't just affect you, it affects everyone connected to you.

## WHY THIS CHAPTER COMES NOW

This chapter comes after identity and choice for a reason. You can know who you are, and you can decide to change. But if your emotions stay unaddressed, they will sabotage your decisions.

Anger will override clarity.
Pain will distort judgment.
Unhealed wounds will keep pulling you back.
Healing makes you stable.

## THE ROLE OF FAITH IN HEALING

Faith doesn't erase pain, but it does give you the courage to face it. God asks you to bring what hurt you into the light so it can stop controlling you from the shadows.

Healing is not forgetting. Healing is freedom from being triggered by what you remember.

## THE TRUTH TO CARRY FORWARD

You are not wrong for feeling what you feel. But you are responsible for what you do with it.

Anger doesn't make you powerful. Awareness does. Healing doesn't make you weak. It makes you whole.

And the man who can feel, reflect, and respond with control is the man who can lead his life rather than be led by his pain. That's the work.

And this chapter is where it begins.

# GROWTH WORK — CHAPTER FOUR

## EMOTIONS, ANGER, AND HEALING

It's time to look beneath your reactions. You don't have to impress anyone.

You just have to be honest.

## PART ONE: NAMING WHAT YOU FEEL

Most men were taught how to react, not how to identify emotions. This section slows that down.

1. **When you get angry, what usually triggers it?**

   Think about specific situations:

- Disrespect
- Feeling ignored
- Being challenged
- Being misunderstood
- Feeling out of control

______________________________________________

______________________________________________

______________________________________________

______________________________________________

______________________________________________

2. **What emotion usually comes before the anger?**

   Anger is often covering something else.

   Examples: hurt, fear, embarrassment, disappointment, sadness.

## PART TWO: YOUR ANGER PATTERN

Anger usually follows a pattern.

3. **When anger shows up, how do you usually respond?**

   Be honest about what you do — not what you wish you did.

   Examples:

   - Explode verbally
   - Shut down
   - Get physical
   - Hold grudges
   - Avoid people
   - Self-sabotage

4. **What has your anger cost you in the past?**

   Think about relationships, opportunities, freedom, trust, or peace.

## PART THREE: WHAT YOU NEVER GOT TO PROCESS

Some emotions were never given space.

5. **What experiences from your past still affect how you react today?**

   These could include:

   - Abandonment
   - Violence
   - Loss
   - Betrayal
   - Neglect
   - Humiliation

6. **At the time, how were you expected to deal with those experiences?**

   Examples:

   - "Man up."
   - "Get over it."
   - "Don't talk about it."
   - "Handle it yourself."

## PART FOUR: REACTION VS. RESPONSE

Growth happens in the pause.

7. **Think about a recent moment where you reacted instead of responding.**

   What happened?

   What did you feel?

   What did you do?

8. **If you had paused, what might you have done differently?**

   This is not about regret — it's about awareness.

## PART FIVE: THE WORK OF HEALING

Healing doesn't erase the past. It changes how the past controls you.

9. **What emotions do you avoid feeling the most?**

   Why do you think that is?

10. **What do you believe would happen if you allowed yourself to feel those emotions safely?**

## PART SIX: TAKING RESPONSIBILITY

Healing starts with ownership.

11. **Finish this sentence honestly:**

    "My anger is trying to protect me from..."

12. **Finish this sentence intentionally:**

    "If I learn to respond instead of react, my life can..."

## CLOSING REFLECTION

Read what you wrote.

Notice patterns.

You are not weak for feeling or needing healing. But you are responsible for what you do with your emotions. Anger is a signal, not a command. And learning to respond instead of react is one of the strongest moves a man can make.

Carry that forward.

# CHAPTER FIVE

# PURPOSE AND VISION — WHAT ARE YOU LIVING FOR?

Let me say this first, because it needs to be said clearly.

Purpose is not a job. Purpose is not money or a title.

Purpose is not applause.

Those things can be part of your life, but they are not why you exist.

A lot of men feel lost not because they're incapable, but because they've been chasing outcomes instead of meaning. They've been busy surviving, reacting, and getting through the day without ever stopping to ask the deeper question: What am I actually living for?

This chapter asks you to slow down and answer that question honestly.

## WHY PURPOSE GETS CONFUSED

When you grow up in survival mode, vision shrinks. You don't think five years ahead. You think about tonight. You think about this week. You think about how to get through what's in front of you.

There's nothing wrong with survival — it keeps you alive. But when survival becomes permanent, purpose gets postponed.

A lot of us learned to measure success by:

- How much money we could make

- How fast we could get it
- How much respect we could command
- How untouchable we could feel

Those measurements make sense in survival mode. They just don't satisfy the soul.

## PURPOSE VS. ESCAPE

Here's a hard truth. A lot of things we chase aren't purpose; they are escape.

Money can be an escape. Status can be escape. Even being busy can be an escape. Escape keeps you moving, but it doesn't tell you where you're going.

Purpose gives direction. And without direction, effort gets wasted.

## WHY VISION MATTERS

Vision is purpose with clarity. Purpose answers why you're here. Vision answers where you're headed.

Without vision, life becomes reactive. You respond to whatever shows up. You take whatever opportunity comes without asking if it aligns with who you're becoming. That's how people end up busy but unfulfilled.

Vision doesn't mean you have every detail figured out. It means you have a direction that guides your decisions.

## CASE STUDY: THE CROSSROADS

Here's a familiar situation.

Two men both say they want more out of life.

One man keeps chasing whatever opportunity comes his way. Fast money, quick wins, short-term relief. He stays moving, but he's always starting over. Nothing builds.

The other man steps back and asks harder questions:

- What do I want my life to stand for?
- Who do I want to impact?
- What kind of man do I want to become?

He chooses a slower path. It doesn't look impressive at first. Progress feels quiet. Sometimes it feels like he's behind. But over time, something changes.

His decisions start lining up. His energy becomes focused. His choices begin to build on each other.

One man is busy.

The other is intentional.

Only one is living with vision.

## HOW PURPOSE GETS REVEALED

Purpose is not something you invent. It's something you uncover.

It shows up through:

- What you're drawn to
- What breaks your heart
- What you've survived
- What people naturally come to you for
- What you can't ignore, even when you try

A lot of men miss their purpose because they're waiting for something dramatic. But purpose often grows out of pain, experience, and responsibility.

## WHY PAIN IS OFTEN CONNECTED TO PURPOSE

This part is uncomfortable, but it's real. The things that hurt you didn't just wound you — they shaped you. They gave you insight and empathy. They gave you understanding that other people don't have.

Purpose often lives right next to pain. Not to glorify suffering, but to redeem it.

What you've been through is not meaningless.

It's raw material.

## PURPOSE REQUIRES COMMITMENT

Here's something that needs to be said honestly. Purpose isn't exciting every day.

Sometimes it's repetitive. Sometimes it's lonely or frustrating. But purpose gives meaning to sacrifice. When you know why you're doing something, endurance becomes possible.

Without purpose, discipline feels like punishment.

With purpose, discipline feels like an investment.

## WHY THIS CHAPTER COMES AFTER HEALING

This chapter comes now for a reason. You can't see clearly when you're emotionally bleeding. Healing creates space. Space creates clarity. Clarity reveals purpose.

Once emotions are addressed, vision can grow without being distorted by anger, fear, or pain.

## FAITH AND PURPOSE

God rarely shows the whole path at once. He reveals enough for the next step. Faith gives you direction, and purpose unfolds as you walk. That requires trust.

And trust requires movement.

## THE TRUTH TO CARRY FORWARD

You were not created just to survive.

You were created to live with intention.

Purpose gives your life weight, and vision gives your life direction. When you start living for something bigger than survival, everything changes.

Not overnight and not easily. But meaningfully.

That's the work of this chapter.

# GROWTH WORK — CHAPTER FIVE

## PURPOSE AND VISION: WHAT ARE YOU LIVING FOR?

You don't need a perfect plan to find your purpose. You just need honesty. Because true purpose requires clarity.

## PART ONE: WHAT YOU'VE BEEN CHASING

Before you can understand purpose, you have to be honest about what you've been living for.

1. **Up until now, what has driven most of your decisions?**

   Examples:

   - Money
   - Survival
   - Respect
   - Approval
   - Comfort
   - Avoiding pain
   - Not wanting to feel behind

   ______________________________________________

   ______________________________________________

   ______________________________________________

   ______________________________________________

2. **Which of those things helped you survive but didn't truly satisfy you?**

## PART TWO: PURPOSE VS. ESCAPE

Not everything we chase is purpose. Sometimes it's escape.

3. **What activities or habits do you use to avoid thinking about your future?**

   Be honest. This is awareness, not shame.

4. **When things get quiet, what thoughts or questions usually come up?**

## PART THREE: CLUES TO YOUR PURPOSE

Purpose leaves clues.

5. **What are you naturally drawn to, even when there's no reward attached?**

   Examples:

   - Teaching
   - Protecting others
   - Creating
   - Fixing things
   - Encouraging
   - Leading
   - Problem-solving

   ______________________________

   ______________________________

   ______________________________

   ______________________________

   ______________________________

6. **What problems in the world or your community bother you the most?**

   Why do you think those affect you personally?

   ______________________________

   ______________________________

   ______________________________

   ______________________________

   ______________________________

## PART FOUR: PAIN AS INFORMATION

Your pain holds information.

7. **What experiences from your past shaped you the most?**

   These can include loss, mistakes, trauma, or responsibilities you had to carry early.

   ______________________________________________

   ______________________________________________

   ______________________________________________

   ______________________________________________

   ______________________________________________

8. **How could those experiences help someone else if you used them with intention?**

   ______________________________________________

   ______________________________________________

   ______________________________________________

   ______________________________________________

   ______________________________________________

## PART FIVE: VISION — LIFTING YOUR EYES

Vision requires direction.

9. **If your life were moving in the right direction, what would be different six months from now?**

   Think about:

   - Your mindset
   - Your habits

- Your relationships
- Your daily structure

_______________________________________________

_______________________________________________

_______________________________________________

_______________________________________________

_______________________________________________

10. **What kind of man do you want people to experience when they interact with you?**

    Not what you do — who you are.

_______________________________________________

_______________________________________________

_______________________________________________

_______________________________________________

_______________________________________________

## PART SIX: COMMITTING TO DIRECTION

Purpose starts with intention.

11. **Finish this sentence honestly:**

    "Right now, my life feels meaningful when I..."

_______________________________________________

_______________________________________________

_______________________________________________

_______________________________________________

12. **Finish this sentence intentionally:**

"I believe my purpose includes..."

(This does not have to be perfect or final.)

## CLOSING REFLECTION

Read what you wrote.

Notice patterns.

You don't need a complete vision yet. But now you know this: You were not created just to get through life. You were created to live with intention.

Purpose gives meaning to discipline, and vision gives direction to effort.

Carry that clarity with you as you move forward.

# CHAPTER SIX

# RELATIONSHIPS, RESPECT, AND FAMILY — HOW DO YOU SHOW UP FOR OTHERS?

Let me say something straight. A lot of men want respect, but they haven't learned how to give it. A lot of men want strong relationships, but they haven't learned how to show up consistently.

And a lot of men say "family means everything," but don't realize that family requires work, patience, and responsibility.

Be mindful in your presence. Because how you treat people, especially the ones closest to you, reveals who you really are.

## WHY RELATIONSHIPS ARE A MIRROR

Relationships don't just connect you to others. They reflect you back to yourself.

How you handle disagreement and deal with disappointment. How you respond when you feel misunderstood and treat people when you're stressed. All of that shows up in a relationship.

You can hide a lot of things when you're alone, but you can't hide them when you're in a relationship. That's why relationships are often where growth gets tested.

## WHAT RESPECT REALLY MEANS

Respect is often misunderstood.

A lot of us grew up thinking respect meant fear, silence, or control. That if people didn't challenge you, they respected you. If people moved out of the way, you were respected.

But that kind of respect doesn't last.

Genuine respect is built through:

- Consistency
- Integrity
- Accountability
- How you treat people when you have power
- How you respond when you don't get your way

Respect isn't demanded. It's demonstrated.

## HOW WE LEARNED RELATIONSHIP PATTERNS

Most of us didn't get a healthy blueprint for relationships.

We learned from what we saw:

- Who argued
- Who disappeared
- Who held grudges
- Who avoided responsibility
- Who dominated instead of listened

So we copied patterns — not because they were right, but because they were familiar.

And familiarity can feel like truth, even when it's unhealthy.

## CASE STUDY: THE MISUNDERSTANDING

This is a common one.

A man feels disrespected by someone close to him — a partner, a family member, a friend. Words are taken the wrong way. Tone feels off. Old feelings get triggered.

He doesn't pause or ask questions. He assumes intent.

His response is sharp. Defensive. Dismissive. The conversation escalates. Trust takes a hit. The relationship pulls back.

Another man feels the same thing — the same tension, the same trigger. But he slows down. He asks for clarity. He listens instead of loading his response.

The conversation isn't perfect. It's uncomfortable. But respect is protected.

One man chose reaction. The other chose responsibility.

Both felt the same emotion.

Only one preserved the relationship.

## FAMILY AND UNFINISHED BUSINESS

Family relationships are complicated. They come with history and expectations. They come with wounds that go back years.

A lot of men carry unresolved feelings toward parents, siblings, or caregivers — anger, disappointment, confusion, grief. And when those feelings aren't addressed, they show up sideways in other relationships.

You're not weak for having family issues. But you are responsible for how you carry them forward.

## SHOWING UP CONSISTENTLY

Being present does not require grand gestures. Just be consistent.

Call when you say you will. Do what you said you'd do. Own mistakes without excuses and listen without interrupting.

Be accountable even when it's uncomfortable.

Consistency builds trust, and trust builds respect.

And respect holds relationships together.

## BOUNDARIES ARE PART OF RESPECT

Here's something that often gets missed.

Respect includes boundaries. Loving someone doesn't mean letting them cross lines, and respecting yourself doesn't mean disrespecting others. Healthy boundaries protect relationships; they don't destroy them.

A man who knows how to set boundaries is a man who knows his value.

## WHY THIS CHAPTER COMES AFTER PURPOSE

Once you start walking with purpose, relationships change. Some people support you. Some people resist the change. Most relationships need adjustment.

This chapter helps you navigate that without burning bridges or losing yourself.

Purpose without relational wisdom leads to isolation.

Relationships without purpose lead to stagnation.

You need both.

## THE ROLE OF FAITH IN RELATIONSHIPS

Faith doesn't make relationships easy, but it does make them intentional.

It teaches humility instead of ego and listening instead of reacting. Forgiveness instead of holding score.

Faith gives you a standard for how you treat people. Not based on how they treat you, but based on who you're becoming.

## THE TRUTH TO CARRY FORWARD

How you treat people matters. Not just when things are easy, but when things are tense. Strong men don't dominate relationships. They steward them. They show up and take responsibility.

They protect respect — including their own.

That's what builds family and legacy.

And that's the work of this chapter.

# GROWTH WORK — CHAPTER SIX

## RELATIONSHIPS, RESPECT, AND FAMILY

Think about how you show up. Not what you expect from others. Not what people did to you.

What you bring into relationships.

Take your time.

## PART ONE: HOW YOU EXPERIENCE RESPECT

Before we talk about relationships, we have to talk about respect.

1. **What makes you feel respected?**

   Think about actions, not words.

2. **What makes you feel disrespected?**

   Be specific. Think about tone, behavior, or situations.

## PART TWO: HOW YOU GIVE RESPECT

Respect goes both ways.

3. **When you feel disrespected, how do you usually respond?**

   Examples:

   - Shut down
   - Get defensive
   - Get aggressive
   - Withdraw
   - Say nothing and hold resentment

4. **How might your response affect the relationship long-term?**

## PART THREE: FAMILY DYNAMICS

Family shapes us — whether we want it to or not.

5. **Who in your family relationships feels unresolved for you?**

   This could be a parent, sibling, caregiver, or extended family member.

   ______________________________________________

   ______________________________________________

   ______________________________________________

   ______________________________________________

   ______________________________________________

6. **What emotions come up when you think about that relationship?**

   Examples:

   - Anger
   - Disappointment
   - Hurt
   - Guilt
   - Confusion
   - Sadness

   ______________________________________________

   ______________________________________________

   ______________________________________________

   ______________________________________________

   ______________________________________________

## PART FOUR: PATTERNS YOU CARRY

What you learned shows up later.

7. **What relationship patterns did you grow up seeing?**

   Examples:

   - Avoidance
   - Explosive arguments
   - Silence
   - Control
   - Disrespect
   - Loyalty without accountability

   ______________________________

   ______________________________

   ______________________________

   ______________________________

   ______________________________

8. **Which of those patterns do you see in yourself today?**

   ______________________________

   ______________________________

   ______________________________

   ______________________________

   ______________________________

## PART FIVE: BOUNDARIES AND RESPONSIBILITY

Healthy relationships require boundaries.

9. **Where do you struggle most with boundaries?**

   Examples:

   - Saying no
   - Letting people guilt you
   - Overgiving
   - Allowing disrespect
   - Avoiding hard conversations

   ______________________________

   ______________________________

   ______________________________

   ______________________________

   ______________________________

10. **What boundary would protect your peace and your growth right now?**

   ______________________________

   ______________________________

   ______________________________

   ______________________________

   ______________________________

## PART SIX: SHOWING UP DIFFERENTLY

Growth shows up in behavior.

11. **What is one relationship where you need to show up differently?**

    Not perfectly, but differently.

    ____________________

    ____________________

    ____________________

    ____________________

    ____________________

12. **What is one action you can take to build trust in that relationship?**

    Think small and consistent.

    ____________________

    ____________________

    ____________________

    ____________________

    ____________________

## CLOSING REFLECTION

Read what you wrote.

Notice where responsibility shows up.

Notice where honesty showed up.

Notice where growth is possible.

Strong relationships are not built on control or fear.

They are built on:

- Respect
- Accountability
- Consistency
- Presence

How you treat people today shapes the legacy you leave tomorrow.

Carry that forward.

# CHAPTER SEVEN

# FAITH, MINDSET AND TRANSFORMATION — HOW DO YOU CHANGE FROM THE INSIDE OUT?

A lot of people try to change their life by changing their situation. A new environment, new routine, or new circle.

Those things matter, but they don't last if the mindset stays the same. Fundamental transformation doesn't start on the outside. It begins on the inside.

Faith reshapes your thinking, and your thinking reshapes your life.

## WHY MINDSET MATTERS MORE THAN CIRCUMSTANCES

Two people can go through the same situation and come out completely different.

One grows. One repeats the cycle.

The difference isn't intelligence. It isn't talent or luck. It's mindset. Mindset is the lens through which you see life.

It determines:

- How you interpret setbacks
- How you respond to pressure
- What you believe is possible

- Whether you quit or keep going

If your mindset doesn't change, your behavior will eventually drift back to what's familiar, even if it's destructive.

## HOW FAITH AND MINDSET CONNECT

Faith is more than a belief in God. It's about belief in possibility.

Faith teaches you that:

- You are not defined by your past
- You are not limited by your environment
- You are not stuck in who you used to be

Faith interrupts hopeless thinking. It introduces a different narrative: That growth is possible. That healing is possible, and transformation is real.

But faith doesn't work without discipline. Faith gives direction, but mindset determines direction.

## CASE STUDY: SAME LIFE, DIFFERENT THINKING

Two men are facing the same reality.

Same environment. Same pressure. Same past mistakes.

One man believes:

"This is just how my life is."

"People like me don't really change."

"I'll try, but it probably won't last."

The other man believes:

"I've made mistakes, but I'm not finished."

"This season doesn't define my future."

"I can build something different."

They both struggle, and they both get tired.

They both get tested, but only one keeps moving forward. Not because life is easier, but because his thinking is different.

Transformation doesn't happen when life gets lighter. It happens when your mindset gets stronger.

## WHY OLD THINKING IS HARD TO LET GO

Old thinking is comfortable, even when it hurts. Familiar pain feels safer than unfamiliar growth and negative self-talk.

Survival habits, defensive attitudes, and low expectations. Those patterns once protected you. Now they limit you. Growth requires unlearning, and unlearning takes humility.

## THE ROLE OF DISCIPLINE IN TRANSFORMATION

Transformation takes consistency.

It shows up in:

- What you feed your mind
- Who you listen to
- What you practice daily
- How you respond when nobody's watching

Discipline is structure that supports change. Without discipline, motivation fades. With discipline, progress compounds.

## RENEWING YOUR MIND

Transformation requires replacing old thoughts with truth. That doesn't happen once. It happens daily.

You catch the thought. You challenge the lie. And you choose a better response.

This is work, and it takes practice. And it is also growth. Faith helps you believe change is possible.

Mindset helps you live it out.

## WHY TRANSFORMATION TAKES TIME

Real change doesn't rush. It's layered and tested. It's reinforced over time.

There will be moments when you feel like nothing is changing. That's usually when something is changing beneath the surface.

Consistency beats intensity every time.

## FROM SURVIVAL TO STEWARDSHIP

Survival mindset says: "Get through today."
Transformation mindset says, "How do I build for tomorrow?"
You stop reacting and start planning. You stop avoiding and start addressing.
That shift is what turns survival into stewardship — of your mind, your choices, and your future.

## THE TRUTH TO CARRY FORWARD

You don't change by wishing. You change by renewing. Faith opens the door, and mindset walks through it. Discipline keeps you moving.

Transformation requires becoming intentional. And once your mind changes, your life follows.

That's the work of this chapter.

# GROWTH WORK — CHAPTER SEVEN

## FAITH, MINDSET, AND TRANSFORMATION

Transformation starts with awareness. Before behavior changes, thinking must change.

Take your time with this work.

## PART ONE: YOUR CURRENT MINDSET

Let's start with honesty.

1. **When life gets hard, what is your first thought?**

   Examples:

   - "Here we go again."
   - "This always happens to me."
   - "I can't get ahead."
   - "I'll try, but it won't last."

2. **Where do you think that thought came from?**

   Family patterns, environment, trauma, past failure, fear, etc.

   _______________________________________________

   _______________________________________________

   _______________________________________________

   _______________________________________________

   _______________________________________________

## PART TWO: IDENTIFYING OLD BELIEFS

Old beliefs often feel true because they're familiar.

3. **What beliefs about yourself have been holding you back?**

   Examples:

   - "I'm not smart enough."
   - "People like me don't change."
   - "I always mess things up."

   _______________________________________________

   _______________________________________________

   _______________________________________________

   _______________________________________________

   _______________________________________________

4. **How have those beliefs affected your choices?**

   _______________________________________________

   _______________________________________________

   _______________________________________________

## PART THREE: FAITH AND POSSIBILITY

Faith introduces a different story.

5. **What does faith say is possible for your life?**

   Be honest.

6. **What would change if you actually believed that was true?**

## PART FOUR: RENEWING YOUR THINKING

Mindset change requires replacement.

7. **Identify one negative thought you need to interrupt.**

8. **Write a truth that challenges that thought.**

9. **How will you remind yourself of this truth daily?**

Examples:

- Writing it down
- Prayer
- Repeating it
- Talking to someone accountable

## PART FIVE: DISCIPLINE AND DAILY PRACTICE

Transformation happens through repetition.

10. **What daily habit would support a healthier mindset?**

    Examples:

    - Prayer or reflection
    - Reading
    - Journaling
    - Exercise
    - Limiting negative input

11. **What usually gets in the way of consistency for you?**

## PART SIX: COMMITTING TO CHANGE

Transformation requires commitment.

12. **Finish this sentence honestly:**

    "Right now, the biggest mindset shift I need is..."

    ______________________________________________

    ______________________________________________

    ______________________________________________

    ______________________________________________

    ______________________________________________

13. **Finish this sentence intentionally:**

    "I am committed to renewing my mind by..."

    ______________________________________________

    ______________________________________________

    ______________________________________________

    ______________________________________________

    ______________________________________________

## CLOSING REFLECTION

Read what you wrote.

Notice patterns.

Notice resistance.

Faith opens the door. Mindset walks through it. Discipline keeps you moving.

Transformation happens one thought at a time.

Carry that forward.

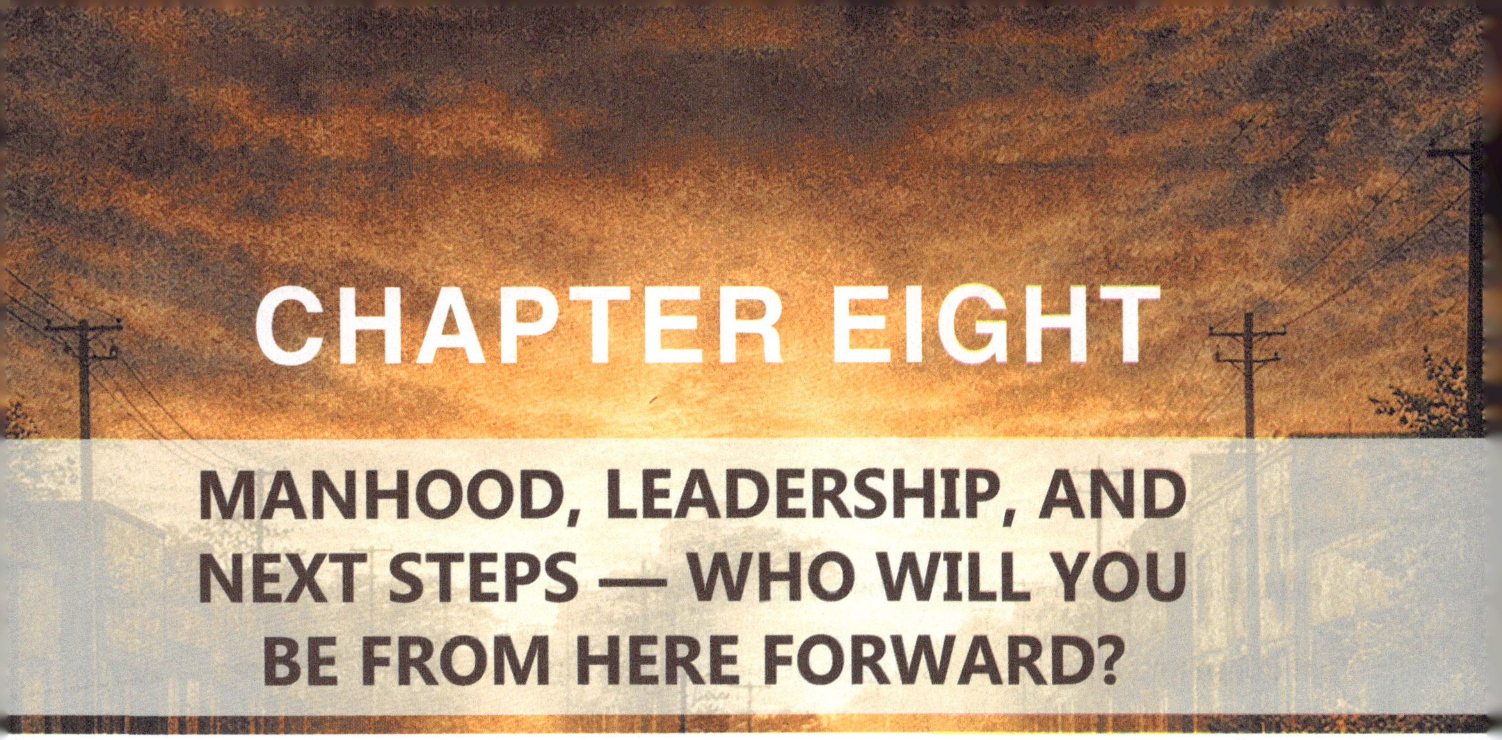

# CHAPTER EIGHT

# MANHOOD, LEADERSHIP, AND NEXT STEPS — WHO WILL YOU BE FROM HERE FORWARD?

If you've made it this far, you need to hear this clearly:

You are no longer the same man who started this journey. Awareness changes responsibility, and once you see yourself clearly, you can't unsee it.

Once you understand your patterns, you can't pretend you don't know them.

And once you recognize your power to choose, you can't blame everything on circumstance anymore.

That's where manhood begins.

At responsibility.

## WHAT MANHOOD REALLY IS

Manhood isn't age.

Manhood isn't strength.

Manhood isn't money, dominance, or reputation.

Manhood is ownership.

Ownership of:

- Your choices
- Your reactions
- Your growth
- Your impact on others

A man doesn't run from responsibility; he rises to it.

That doesn't mean you don't struggle. It means you stop hiding behind excuses.

## THE SHIFT FROM SURVIVAL TO LEADERSHIP

Most of us were raised to survive.

*Get through the day.*

*Protect yourself.*

*Don't show weakness.*

*Handle problems alone.*

Survival teaches defense, but leadership requires vision. And leadership means being accountable.

The moment you decide, "My life matters enough to live intentionally," you step into leadership — whether anyone is watching or not.

## CASE STUDY: THE FORK IN THE ROAD

Two men complete the same journey.

Both learn. Both reflect, and both feel motivated.

One man walks away and says, "That was good."

He feels inspired, but he doesn't change his habits. He understands, but he doesn't apply. Life slowly pulls him back into old routines.

The other man walks away and says: "I can't go back to who I was."

He doesn't rush. He doesn't try to fix everything at once. But he commits to doing one thing differently every day.

Six months later, their lives look different. Not because one knew more, but because one took responsibility.

Leadership always shows up in action.

## WHY LEADERSHIP STARTS WITH SELF

Before you lead anyone else, you must lead yourself.

That means:

- Regulating your emotions
- Managing your time
- Being honest about your weaknesses
- Building discipline without applause

Self-leadership is quiet. It's consistent, and it's powerful.

A man who can lead himself can be trusted with influence.

## THE ROLE OF COMMUNITY IN MANHOOD

No strong man stands alone.

Isolation is not strength — it's vulnerability.

Healthy men build:

- Accountability

- Brotherhood
- Mentorship
- Support systems

Leadership grows in community. Iron sharpens iron.

If you want to grow, you need people who will challenge you — not just comfort you.

## WHAT LEGACY REALLY MEANS

Legacy isn't what people say about you when you're gone. Legacy is what people experience from you while you're here.

How you show up.
How you treat people.
What you stand for.
What you pass down.

Legacy is built daily, not dramatically. And whether you realize it or not, someone is watching how you live.

## NEXT STEPS: WALKING IT OUT

This journey doesn't end here.

It continues in:

- The choices you make when nobody's watching
- The boundaries you keep
- The discipline you maintain
- The honesty you practice
- The faith you live out

You don't need to become a different man overnight. You need to become a more intentional one.

## A FINAL WORD

You were not born to repeat cycles. You were not created to stay stuck or live without purpose.

You were born to grow. You were born to lead and to become.

This work has shown you who you are. Now life will test who you choose to be.

Choose wisely.

Choose courage.

Choose responsibility.

Choose growth.

And walk forward like the man you're becoming.

# GROWTH WORK — CHAPTER EIGHT

## MANHOOD, LEADERSHIP, AND NEXT STEPS

You've done the reflection. Now comes the responsibility.

Take this seriously. This is about how you will live from here forward.

## PART ONE: OWNING YOUR GROWTH

Manhood begins with ownership.

1. **What is one area of your life where you can no longer blame anyone else?**

   ______________________________

   ______________________________

   ______________________________

   ______________________________

   ______________________________

2. **What excuse have you been using that you're ready to release?**

   ______________________________

   ______________________________

   ______________________________

   ______________________________

   ______________________________

## PART TWO: SELF-LEADERSHIP

Leadership starts with how you lead yourself.

3. **Where do you need more discipline in your life right now?**

   Examples:

   - Time
   - Emotions
   - Money
   - Communication
   - Habits

4. **What is one daily habit you will commit to that supports your growth?**

## PART THREE: YOUR CIRCLE AND SUPPORT

No man grows alone.

5. **Who can hold you accountable moving forward?**

   Name someone specific.

6. **How will you invite accountability instead of avoiding it?**

## PART FOUR: LEGACY AND IMPACT

Think beyond yourself.

7. **What kind of man do you want people to experience when they encounter you?**

8. **Who do you want your life to positively impact?**

_______________________________________________

_______________________________________________

_______________________________________________

_______________________________________________

_______________________________________________

## PART FIVE: YOUR NEXT RIGHT STEPS

Growth happens through action.

9. **What is one decision you will make differently starting today?**

_______________________________________________

_______________________________________________

_______________________________________________

_______________________________________________

_______________________________________________

10. **What is one boundary you will maintain to protect your progress?**

_______________________________________________

_______________________________________________

_______________________________________________

_______________________________________________

_______________________________________________

## PART SIX: COMMITMENT STATEMENT

This is your moment of commitment.

11. **Complete this statement honestly:**

    "From this point forward, I commit to becoming a man who..."

    ______________________________

    ______________________________

    ______________________________

    ______________________________

12. **Sign and date your commitment.**

    Name: ______________________________

    Date: ______________________________

    ______________________________

    ______________________________

    ______________________________

    ______________________________

## CLOSING REFLECTION

Read what you wrote.

This is not a promise of perfection. This is a decision to be intentional.

Manhood is not proven in words. It's revealed in consistent action.

Carry this commitment with you.

The journey doesn't end here — it begins now.